THIS BOOK BELONGS TO

THANK YOU

**DEAR
FRIEND!**

Thank you for choosing
this book. We sincerely
hope that it will give you
joy as you color these
pages.

If you could spare two minutes
of your time to write an Amazon review,
we would be really grateful and very
happy to read it. It helps us improve and
bring more beautiful illustrations for
our audiences, and helps potential
buyers to make confident decisions

Colored pencils or pens are best suited
for this paper. But if you prefer to use
markers or paints, please make sure
you put a few sheets of paper under the
page you are coloring in to avoid
smudges on the bottom pages.

**ENJOY
COLORING!**

Illustrations & design:

Alina Plat

CHECK OUT ALLY.PLT
ON SOCIAL MEDIA

Subscribe to my Direct.me page to get my

FREE DIGITAL COLORING BOOK!

Includes 30 pages from ALLY PLT best sellers

AND MORE

NO EXTRA COST

NO DIFFICULTY

https://direct.me/allyplt

S A M P L E :

Thank you for choosing ALLY PLT coloring books

CHECK OUT MORE BOOKS FROM US :

Made in the USA
Columbia, SC
28 September 2023

23509006R00030